Jesus Christ and Mythology

Also by Rudolf Bultmann

JESUS AND THE WORD
THEOLOGY OF THE NEW TESTAMENT, 2 VOLUMES
THIS WORLD AND THE BEYOND

Jesus Christ
and Mythology

RUDOLF BULTMANN

CHARLES SCRIBNER'S SONS New York

Contents

Preface

This small volume contains the Shaffer Lectures which I delivered in October 1951 at Yale University Divinity School and the Cole Lectures, delivered at Vanderbilt University in November 1951. The content of the Shaffer Lectures and of the Cole Lectures was partly identical.

Some of the lectures were also given at other institutions: at Wellesley College, Andover Newton Theological School and Boston University School of Theology; Chicago University (Federated Theological Faculty) and Maywood Lutheran Seminary; Princeton Seminary and Drew Seminary; Hartford Theological Seminary; Emory University; Union Theological Seminary (New York) and Crozer Theological Seminary.

I remember with pleasure my visits to these schools

and am grateful for the kindness with which I was received everywhere, and for all I have learned in numerous discussions with colleagues.

I am especially indebted to Yale University and to Vanderbilt University for inviting me to deliver, respectively, the Shaffer Lectures and the Cole Lectures.

Finally, I express my thanks to Professor Paul Schubert who has prepared the manuscript for publication, and to Professor Erich Dinkler, Mr. D. E. H. Whitely, and Mr. Victor P. Furnish, who have assisted him at various stages of the work.

RUDOLF BULTMANN
MARBURG, APRIL, 1958

Jesus Christ and Mythology

I

The Message of Jesus and
the Problem of Mythology

·1·

The heart of the preaching of Jesus Christ is the Kingdom of God. During the nineteenth century exegesis and theology understood the Kingdom of God as a spiritual community consisting of men joined together by obedience to the will of God which ruled in their wills. By such obedience they sought to enlarge the sphere of His rule in the world. They were building, it was said, the Kingdom of God as a realm which is spiritual but within the world, active and effective in this world, unfolding in the history of this world.

The year 1892 saw the publication of *The Preaching of Jesus about the Kingdom of God* by Johannes Weiss.

This epoch-making book refuted the interpretation which was hitherto generally accepted. Weiss showed that the Kingdom of God is not immanent in the world and does not grow as part of the world's history, but is rather eschatological; i.e., the Kingdom of God transcends the historical order. It will come into being not through the moral endeavour of man, but solely through the supernatural action of God. God will suddenly put an end to the world and to history, and He will bring in a new world, the world of eternal blessedness.

This conception of the Kingdom of God was not an invention of Jesus. It was a conception familiar in certain circles of Jews who were waiting for the end of this world. This picture of the eschatological drama was drawn in Jewish apocalyptic literature, of which the book of Daniel is the earliest still extant. The preaching of Jesus is distinguished from the typical apocalyptic pictures of the eschatological drama and of the blessedness of the coming new age in so far as Jesus refrained from drawing detailed pictures. He confined himself to the statement that the Kingdom of God will come and that men must be prepared to face the coming judgment. Otherwise he shared the eschatological expectations of his contemporaries. That is why he taught his disciples to pray,

Hallowed be thy name,
Thy Kingdom come,
Thy will be done on earth as it is in heaven.

Jesus expected that this would take place soon, in the immediate future, and he said that the dawning of that

12

age could already be perceived in the signs and wonders which he performed, especially in his casting out of demons. Jesus envisaged the inauguration of the Kingdom of God as a tremendous cosmic drama. The Son of Man will come with the clouds of heaven, the dead will be raised and the day of judgment will arrive; for the righteous the time of bliss will begin, whereas the damned will be delivered to the torments of hell.

When I began to study theology, theologians as well as laymen were excited and frightened by the theories of Johannes Weiss. I remember that Julius Kaftan, my teacher in dogmatics in Berlin, said: "If Johannes Weiss is right and the conception of the Kingdom of God is an eschatological one, then it is impossible to make use of this conception in dogmatics." But in the following years the theologians, J. Kaftan among them, became convinced that Weiss was correct. Perhaps I may here refer to Albert Schweitzer who carried the theory of Weiss to extremes. He maintains that not only the preaching and the self-consciousness of Jesus but also his day-to-day conduct of life were dominated by an eschatological expectation which amounted to an all-pervading eschatological dogma.

Today nobody doubts that Jesus' conception of the Kingdom of God is an eschatological one—at least in European theology and, as far as I can see, also among American New Testament scholars. Indeed, it has become more and more clear that the eschatological expectation and hope is the core of the New Testament preaching throughout.

The earliest Christian community understood the

13

Kingdom of God in the same sense as Jesus. It, too, expected the Kingdom of God to come in the immediate future. So Paul, too, thought that he would still be alive when the end of this world was to come and the dead were to be raised. This general conviction is confirmed by the voices of impatience, of anxiety and of doubt which are already audible in the synoptic gospels and which echo a little later and louder, for example, in the Second Epistle of Peter. Christianity has always retained the hope that the Kingdom of God will come in the immediate future, although it has waited in vain. We may cite Mark 9:1, which is not a genuine saying of Jesus but was ascribed to him by the earliest community: "Truly, I say to you, there are some standing here who will not taste death before they see the kingdom of God come with power." Is not the meaning of this verse clear? Though many of the contemporaries of Jesus are already dead, the hope must nevertheless be retained that the Kingdom of God will still come in this generation.

·2·

This hope of Jesus and of the early Christian community was not fulfilled. The same world still exists and history continues. The course of history has refuted mythology. For the conception "Kingdom of God" is mythological, as is the conception of the eschatological drama. Just as mythological are the presuppositions of the expectation of the Kingdom of God, namely, the theory that the world, although created by God, is ruled

14

by the devil, Satan, and that his army, the demons, is the cause of all evil, sin and disease. The whole conception of the world which is presupposed in the preaching of Jesus as in the New Testament generally is mythological; i.e., the conception of the world as being structured in three stories, heaven, earth and hell; the conception of the intervention of supernatural powers in the course of events; and the conception of miracles, especially the conception of the intervention of supernatural powers in the inner life of the soul, the conception that men can be tempted and corrupted by the devil and possessed by evil spirits. This conception of the world we call mythological because it is different from the conception of the world which has been formed and developed by science since its inception in ancient Greece and which has been accepted by all modern men. In this modern conception of the world the cause-and-effect nexus is fundamental. Although modern physical theories take account of chance in the chain of cause and effect in subatomic phenomena, our daily living, purposes and actions are not affected. In any case, modern science does not believe that the course of nature can be interrupted or, so to speak, perforated, by supernatural powers.

The same is true of the modern study of history, which does not take into account any intervention of God or of the devil or of demons in the course of history. Instead, the course of history is considered to be an unbroken whole, complete in itself, though differing from the course of nature because there are in history

15

spiritual powers which influence the will of persons. Granted that not all historical events are determined by physical necessity and that persons are responsible for their actions, nevertheless nothing happens without rational motivation. Otherwise, responsibility would be dissolved. Of course, there are still many superstitions among modern men, but they are exceptions or even anomalies. Modern men take it for granted that the course of nature and of history, like their own inner life and their practical life, is nowhere interrupted by the intervention of supernatural powers.

Then the question inevitably arises: is it possible that Jesus' preaching of the Kingdom of God still has any importance for modern men and the preaching of the New Testament as a whole is still important for modern men? The preaching of the New Testament proclaims Jesus Christ, not only his preaching of the Kingdom of God but first of all his person, which was mythologized from the very beginnings of earliest Christianity. New Testament scholars are at variance as to whether Jesus himself claimed to be the Messiah, the King of the time of blessedness, whether he believed himself to be the Son of Man who would come on the clouds of heaven. If so, Jesus understood himself in the light of mythology. We need not, at this point, decide one way or the other. At any rate, the early Christian community thus regarded him as a mythological figure. It expected him to return as the Son of Man on the clouds of heaven to bring salvation and damnation as judge of the world. His person is viewed in the light of mythology when he is

16

said to have been begotten of the Holy Spirit and born of a virgin, and this becomes clearer still in Hellenistic Christian communities where he is understood to be the Son of God in a metaphysical sense, a great, pre-existent heavenly being who became man for the sake of our redemption and took on himself suffering, even the suffering of the cross. It is evident that such conceptions are mythological, for they were widespread in the mythologies of Jews and Gentiles and then were transferred to the historical person of Jesus. Particularly the conception of the pre-existent Son of God who descended in human guise into the world to redeem mankind is part of the Gnostic doctrine of redemption, and nobody hesitates to call this doctrine mythological. This raises in an acute form the question: *what is the importance of the preaching of Jesus and of the preaching of the New Testament as a whole for modern man?*

For modern man the mythological conception of the world, the conceptions of eschatology, of redeemer and of redemption, are over and done with. Is it possible to expect that we shall make a sacrifice of understanding, *sacrificium intellectus,* in order to accept what we cannot sincerely consider true—merely because such conceptions are suggested by the Bible? Or ought we to pass over those sayings of the New Testament which contain such mythological conceptions and to select other sayings which are not such stumbling-blocks to modern man? In fact, the preaching of Jesus is not confined to eschatological sayings. He proclaimed also the will of God, which is God's demand, the demand for

17

the good. Jesus demands truthfulness and purity, readiness to sacrifice and to love. He demands that the whole man be obedient to God, and he protests against the delusion that one's duty to God can be fulfilled by obeying certain external commandments. If the ethical demands of Jesus are stumbling-blocks to modern man, then it is to his selfish will, not to his understanding, that they are stumbling-blocks.

What follows from all this? Shall we retain the ethical preaching of Jesus and abandon his eschatological preaching? Shall we reduce his preaching of the Kingdom of God to the so-called social gospel? Or is there a third possibility? We must ask whether the eschatological preaching and the mythological sayings as a whole contain a still deeper meaning which is concealed under the cover of mythology. If that is so, let us abandon the mythological conceptions precisely because we want to retain their deeper meaning. This method of interpretation of the New Testament which tries to recover the deeper meaning behind the mythological conceptions I call *de-mythologizing*—an unsatisfactory word, to be sure. Its aim is not to eliminate the mythological statements but to interpret them. It is a method of hermeneutics. The meaning of this method will be best understood when we make clear the meaning of mythology in general.

·3·

It is often said that mythology is a primitive science, the intention of which is to explain phenomena and incidents which are strange, curious, surprising, or frightening, by attributing them to supernatural causes, to gods or to demons. So it is in part, for example, when it attributes phenomena like eclipses of the sun or of the moon to such causes; but there is more than this in mythology. Myths speak about gods and demons as powers on which man knows himself to be dependent, powers whose favor he needs, powers whose wrath he fears. Myths express the knowledge that man is not master of the world and of his life, that the world within which he lives is full of riddles and mysteries and that human life also is full of riddles and mysteries.

Mythology expresses a certain understanding of human existence. It believes that the world and human life have their ground and their limits in a power which is beyond all that we can calculate or control. Mythology speaks about this power inadequately and insufficiently because it speaks about it as if it were a worldly power. It speaks of gods who represent the power beyond the visible, comprehensible world. It speaks of gods as if they were men and of their actions as human actions, although it conceives of the gods as endowed with superhuman power and of their actions as incalculable, as capable of breaking the normal, ordinary order of events. It may be said that myths give to the transcendent reality an immanent, this-worldly objectivity. Myths give worldly objectivity to that which is unworldly. (In German one would say, "Der Mythos objektiviert das Jenseitige zum Diesseitigen.")

19

All this holds true also of the mythological conceptions found in the Bible. According to mythological thinking, God has his domicile in heaven. What is the meaning of this statement? The meaning is quite clear. In a crude manner it expresses the idea that God is beyond the world, that He is transcendent. The thinking which is not yet capable of forming the abstract idea of transcendence expresses its intention in the category of space; the transcendent God is imagined as being at an immense spatial distance, far above the world: for above this world is the world of the stars, of the light which enlightens and makes glad the life of men. When mythological thinking forms the conception of hell, it expresses the idea of the transcendence of evil as the tremendous power which again and again afflicts mankind. The location of hell and of men whom hell has seized is below the earth in darkness, because darkness is tremendous and terrible to men.

These mythological conceptions of heaven and hell are no longer acceptable for modern men since for scientific thinking to speak of "above" and "below" in the universe has lost all meaning, but the idea of the transcendence of God and of evil is still significant.

Another example is the conception of Satan and the evil spirits into whose power men are delivered. This conception rests upon the experience, quite apart from the inexplicable evils arising outside ourselves to which we are exposed, that our own actions are often so puzzling; men are often carried away by their passions and are no longer master of themselves, with the result that inconceivable wickedness breaks forth from them. Again, the conception of Satan as ruler over the world expresses a deep insight, namely, the insight that evil is not only to be found here and there in the world, but that all particular evils make up one single power which in the last analysis grows from the very actions of men, which form an atmosphere, a spiritual tradition, which overwhelms every man. The consequences and effects of our sins become a power dominating us, and we cannot free ourselves from them. Particularly in our day and generation, although we no longer think mythologically, we often speak of demonic powers which rule history, corrupting political and social life. Such language is metaphorical, a figure of speech, but in it is expressed the knowledge, the insight, that the evil for which every man is responsible individually has nevertheless become a power which mysteriously enslaves every member of the human race.

Now the question arises: is it possible to de-mythologize the message of Jesus and the preaching of the early Christian community? Since this preaching was shaped by the eschatological belief, the first question is this: *What is the meaning of eschatology in general?*

II

The Interpretation of

Mythological Eschatology

·1·

In the language of traditional theology eschatology is the doctrine of the last things, and "last" means last in the course of time, that is, the end of the world which is imminent as the future is to our present. But in the actual preaching of the prophets and of Jesus this "last" has a further meaning. As in the conception of heaven the transcendence of God is imagined by means of the category of space, so in the conception of the end of the world, the idea of the transcendence of God is imagined by means of the category of time. However, it is not simply the idea of transcendence as such, but of the importance of the transcendence of God, of God who is

22

never present as a familiar phenomenon but who **is** always the coming God, who is veiled by the unknown future. Eschatological preaching views the present time in the light of the future and it says to men that this present world, the world of nature and history, the world in which we live our lives and make our plans is not the only world; that this world is temporal and transitory, yes, ultimately empty and unreal in the face of eternity.

This understanding is not peculiar to mythical eschatology. It is the knowledge to which Shakespeare gives grand expression:

> The cloud-capp'd towers, the gorgeous palaces,
> The solemn temples, the great globe itself,
> Yea, all which it inherit, shall dissolve,
> And like this insubstantial pageant faded,
> Leave not a rack behind. We are such stuff
> As dreams are made on; and our little life
> Is rounded with a sleep. . . .
>
> *Tempest IV, 1*

It is the same understanding which was current among the Greeks who did not share the eschatology which was common to the prophets and to Jesus. Permit me to quote from a hymn of Pindar:

> Creatures of a day, what is anyone? what is he not?
> Man is but a dream of a shadow.
>
> *Pythian Odes 8, 95-96*

and from Sophocles:

23

> Alas! we living mortals, what are we
> But phantoms all or unsubstantial shades?
>
> *Ajax 125-126*

The perception of the boundary of human life warns men against "presumption" ($ὕβρις$) and calls to "thoughtfulness" and "awe" ($σωφροσύνη$ and $αἰδώς$). "Nothing too much" ($μηδὲν ἄγαν$), "of strength do not boast" ($ἐπὶ ῥώμῃ μὴ καυχῶ$) are sayings of Greek wisdom. Greek tragedy shows the truth of such proverbs in its representations of human destiny. From the soldiers slain in the Battle of Plataeae we should learn, as Aeschylus says, that

> Mortal man needs must not vaunt him overmuch. . . .
> Zeus, of a truth, is a chastiser of overweening pride
> And corrects with heavy hand.
>
> *Persians 820-828*

And again in the *Ajax* of Sophocles Athene says of the mad Ajax,

> Warned by these sights, Odysseus, see that thou
> Utter no boastful word against the gods,
> Nor swell with pride if haply might of arm
> Exalt thee o'er thy fellows, or vast wealth.
> A day can prostrate and a day upraise
> All that is mortal; but the gods approve
> Sobriety and frowardness abhor.
>
> *127-133*

·2·

If it is true that the general human understanding of the insecurity of the present in the face of the future

24

has found expression in eschatological thought, then we must ask, *what is the difference between the Greek and the Biblical understanding?* The Greeks found the immanent power of the beyond, of the gods compared with whom all human affairs are empty, in "destiny." They do not share the mythological conception of eschatology as a cosmic event at the end of time; and it may well be said that Greek thought is more similar to that of modern man than to the Biblical conception, since for modern man mythological eschatology has passed away. It is possible that the Biblical eschatology may rise again. It will not rise in its old mythological form but from the terrifying vision that modern technology, especially atomic science, may bring about the destruction of our earth through the abuse of human science and technology. When we ponder this possibility, we can feel the terror and the anxiety which were evoked by the eschatological preaching of the imminent end of the world. To be sure, that preaching was developed in conceptions which are no longer intelligible today, but they do express the knowledge of the finiteness of the world, and of the end which is imminent to us all because we all are beings of this finite world. This is the insight to which as a rule we turn a blind eye, but which may be brought to light by modern technology. It is precisely the intensity of this insight which explains why Jesus, like the Old Testament prophets, expected the end of the world to occur in the immediate future. The majesty of God and the inescapability of His judgment, and over

25

against these the emptiness of the world and of men were felt with such an intensity that it seemed that the world was at an end, and that the hour of crisis was present. Jesus proclaims the will of God and the responsibility of man, pointing towards the eschatological events, but it is not because he is an eschatologist that he proclaims the will of God. On the contrary, he is an eschatologist because he proclaims the will of God.

The difference between the Biblical and the Greek understanding of the human situation regarding the unknown future can now be seen in a clearer light. It consists in the fact that in the thinking of the prophets and of Jesus the nature of God involves more than simply His omnipotence and His judgment touches not only the man who offends Him by presumption and boasting. For the prophets and for Jesus God is the Holy One, who demands right and righteousness, who demands love of neighbour and who therefore is the judge of all human thoughts and actions. The world is empty not only because it is transitory, but because men have turned it into a place in which evil spreads and sin rules. The end of the world, therefore, is the judgment of God; that is, the eschatological preaching not only brings to consciousness the emptiness of the human situation and calls men, as was the case among the Greeks, to moderation, humility and resignation; it calls men first and foremost to responsibility toward God and to repentance. It calls them to perform the will of God. Thus, the characteristic difference between

26

the eschatological preaching of Jesus and that of the Jewish apocalypses becomes evident. All the pictures of future happiness in which apocalypticism excels are lacking in the preaching of Jesus.

Though in this connection we do not examine other differences between Biblical and Greek thought, as, for instance, the personality of the one holy God, the personal relationship between God and man, and the Biblical belief that God is the creator of the world, we must consider one more important point. The eschatological preaching proclaims the imminent end of the world, not only as the final judgment, but also as the beginning of the time of salvation and of eternal bliss. The end of the world has not only a negative but also a positive meaning. To use nonmythological terms, the finiteness of the world and of man over against the transcendent power of God contains not only warning, but also consolation. Let us ask whether the ancient Greeks also speak in this way about the emptiness of the world and of this-worldly affairs. I think that we can hear such a voice in Euripides' question,

> Who knows if to live is really to die,
> and if to die is to live?
>
> *Frg. 638 (ed. Nauck)*

At the end of his speech to his judges, Socrates says.

> But now the time has come to go away. I go to die and you to live; but which of us goes to the better lot, is known to none but God.
>
> *Apol. 42a*

In a similar vein the Platonic Socrates says,

> If the soul is immortal, we must care for it, not
> only in respect to this time, which we call life,
> but in respect to all time.
>
> *Phaed. 107c.*

Above all, we should think of this famous saying,

> practice dying
> *Phaed. 67e*

This, according to Plato, is the characteristic feature of the life of the philosopher. Death is the separation of the soul from the body. As long as man lives, the soul is bound to the body and to its needs. The philosopher lives his life detaching his soul as much as possible from communion with the body, for the body disturbs the soul and hinders it from attaining the truth. The philosopher looks for cleansing, that is, for release from the body, and so he "gives heed to dying."

If we may call the Platonic hope in life after death an eschatology, then the Christian eschatology agrees with the Platonic eschatology in so far as each expects bliss after death and also in so far as bliss may be called *freedom*. This freedom is for Plato the freedom of the spirit from the body, the freedom of the spirit which can perceive the truth which is the very reality of being; and for Greek thinking, of course, the realm of reality is also the realm of beauty. According to Plato, this transcendent bliss can be described not only in negative and abstract, but also in positive terms. Since the

28

transcendent realm is the realm of truth and truth is to be found in discussion, that is, in dialogue, Plato can picture the transcendent realm positively as a sphere of dialogue. Socrates says that it would be best if he could spend his life in the beyond in examining and exploring as he did on this side. "To converse and associate with them and examine them would be immeasurable happiness" (*Apol.* 41c).

In Christian thinking freedom is not the freedom of a spirit who is satisfied with perceiving the truth; it is the freedom of man to be himself. Freedom is freedom from sin, from wickedness, or as St. Paul says, from the flesh, from the old self, because God is Holy. Thus, obtaining bliss means obtaining grace and righteousness by God's judgment. Moreover, it is impossible to depict the ineffable blessedness of those who are justified, save in symbolic pictures such as a splendid banquet, or in such pictures as the Revelation of John paints. According to Paul, "the kingdom of God does not mean food and drink but righteousness, and peace, and joy in the Holy Spirit" (Rom. 14:17). And Jesus said, "when they rise from the dead, they neither marry nor are given in marriage, but are like angels in heaven" (Mark 12:25). The physical body is replaced by the spiritual body. To be sure, our imperfect knowledge will then become perfect, and then we shall see face to face, as Paul says (I Cor. 13:9-12). But that is by no means knowledge of truth in the Greek sense, but an untroubled relationship with God, as Jesus promised that the pure in heart shall see God (Matt. 5:8).

29

If we can say anything more, it is that the action of God reaches its fulfilment in the glory of God. Thus the Church of God in the present has no other purpose than to praise and glorify God by its conduct (Phil. 1:11) and by its thanksgiving (II Cor. 1:20; 4:15; Rom. 15:6f.). Therefore, the future Church in the state of perfection cannot be thought of otherwise than as a worshiping community which sings hymns of praise and thanksgiving. We can see examples of this in the Revelation of John.

Surely both conceptions of transcendent bliss are mythological, the Platonic conception of bliss as philosophical dialogue as well as the Christian conception of blessedness as worship. Each conception intends to speak about the transcendent world as a world where man reaches the perfection of his true, real essence. This essence can be realized only imperfectly in this world, but nevertheless it determines life in this world as a life of seeking, and longing and yearning.

The difference between the two conceptions is due to different theories of human nature. Plato conceives the realm of spirit as a realm without time and without history because he conceives human nature as not subject to time and history. The Christian conception of the human being is that man is essentially a temporal being, which means that he is an historical being who has a past which shapes his character and who has a future which always brings forth new encounters. Therefore the future after death and beyond this world is a future of the totally new. This is the *totaliter aliter*.

30

Then there will be "a new heaven and a new earth" (Rev. 21:1, II Peter 3:13). The seer of the future Jerusalem hears a voice, "Behold, I make all things new" (Rev. 21:5). Paul and John anticipate this newness. Paul says, "If any one is in Christ, he is a new creation; the old has passed away, behold, the new has come" (II Cor. 5:17), and John says, "I am writing you a new commandment, which is true in him and in you, because the darkness is passing away and the true light is already shining" (I John 2:8). But that newness is not a visible one, for our new life "is hid with Christ in God" (Col. 3:3), "it does not yet appear what we shall be" (I John 3:2). In a certain manner this unknown future is present in the holiness and love which characterize the believers in the Holy Spirit which inspired them, and in the worship of the Church. It cannot be described except in symbolic pictures: "for in this hope we were saved. Now hope that is seen is not hope. For who hopes for what he sees? But if we hope for what we do not see, we wait for it with patience" (Rom. 8:24-5). Therefore, this hope or this faith may be called readiness for the unknown future that God will give. In brief, it means to be open to God's future in the face of death and darkness.

This, then, is the deeper meaning of the mythological preaching of Jesus—to be open to God's future which is really imminent for every one of us; to be prepared for this future which can come as a thief in the night when we do not expect it; to be prepared, because this future will be a judgment on all men who have bound

31

themselves to this world and are not free, not open to God's future.

· 3 ·

The eschatological preaching of Jesus was retained and continued by the early Christian community in its mythological form. But very soon the process of de-mythologizing began, partially with Paul, and radically with John. The decisive step was taken when Paul declared that the turning point from the old world to the new was not a matter of the future but did take place in the coming of Jesus Christ. "But when the time had fully come, God sent forth his Son" (Gal. 4:4). To be sure, Paul still expected the end of the world as a cosmic drama, the *parousia* of Christ on the clouds of heaven, the resurrection from the dead, the final judgment, but with the resurrection of Christ the decisive event has already happened. The Church is the eschatological community of the elect, of the saints who are already justified and are alive because they are in Christ, in Christ who as the second Adam abolished death and brought life and immortality to light through the gospel (Rom. 5:12-14; II Tim. 1:10). "Death is swallowed up in victory" (I Cor. 15:54). Therefore, Paul can say that the expectations and promises of the ancient prophets are fulfilled when the gospel is proclaimed: "Behold, now is the acceptable time [about which Isaiah spoke]; behold, now is the day of salvation" (II Cor. 6:2). The Holy Spirit who was expected as the gift of the time of blessedness has already been given. In this manner the future is anticipated.

This de-mythologizing may be observed in a particular instance. In the Jewish apocalyptic expectations, the expectation of the Messianic kingdom played a role. The Messianic kingdom is, so to speak, an *interregnum* between the old world time (οὖτος ὁ αἰών) and the new age (ὁ μέλλων αἰών). Paul explains this apocalyptic, mythological idea of the Messianic *interregnum*, at the end of which Christ will deliver the Kingdom to God the Father, as the present time between the resurrection of Christ and his coming *parousia* (I Cor. 15:24); that means, the present time of preaching the gospel is really the formerly expected time of the Kingdom of the Messiah. Jesus is now the Messiah, the Lord.

After Paul, John de-mythologized the eschatology in a radical manner. For John the coming and departing of Jesus is the eschatological event. "And this is the judgment, that the light has come into the world, and men loved darkness rather than light, because their deeds were evil" (John 3:19). "Now is the judgment of this world, now shall the ruler of this world be cast out" (12:31). For John the resurrection of Jesus, Pentecost and the *parousia* of Jesus are one and the same event, and those who believe have already eternal life. "He who believes in him is not condemned; he who does not believe is condemned already" (3:18). "He who believes in the Son has eternal life; he who does not obey the Son shall not see life, but the wrath of God rests upon him" (3:36). "Truly, truly, I say to you, the hour is coming, and now is, when the dead will hear the voice of the Son of God, and those who hear will live" (5:25). "I am the resurrection and the life; he

33

who believes in me, though he die, yet shall he live; and whoever lives and believes in me shall never die" (11:25f.).

As in Paul, so in John de-mythologizing may be further observed in a particular instance. In Jewish eschatological expectations we find that the figure of the anti-Christ is a thoroughly mythological figure as it is described, for example, in II Thessalonians (2:7-12). In John false teachers play the role of this mythological figure. Mythology has been transposed into history. These examples show, it seems to me, that de-mythologizing has its beginning in the New Testament itself, and therefore our task of de-mythologizing today is justified.

III

The Christian Message and

the Modern World-View

·1·

An objection often heard against the attempt to de-mythologize is that it takes the modern world-view as the criterion of the interpretation of the Scripture and the Christian message and that Scripture and Christian message are not allowed to say anything that is in contradiction with the modern world-view.

It is, of course, true that de-mythologizing takes the modern world-view as a criterion. To de-mythologize is to reject not Scripture or the Christian message as a whole, but the world-view of Scripture, which is the world-view of a past epoch, which all too often is retained in Christian dogmatics and in the preaching of the Church. To de-mythologize is to deny that the message of Scripture and of the Church is bound to an ancient world-view which is obsolete.

The attempt to de-mythologize begins with this important insight: Christian preaching, in so far as it is preaching of the Word of God by God's command and in His name, does not offer a doctrine which can be accepted either by reason or by a *sacrificium intellectus*. Christian preaching is *kerygma*, that is, a proclamation addressed not to the theoretical reason, but to the hearer as a self. In this manner Paul commends himself to every man's conscience in the sight of God (II Cor. 4:2). De-mythologizing will make clear this function of preaching as a personal message, and in doing so it will eliminate a false stumbling-block and bring into sharp focus the real stumbling-block, the word of the cross.

For the world-view of the Scripture is mythological and is therefore unacceptable to modern man whose thinking has been shaped by science and is therefore no longer mythological. Modern man always makes use of technical means which are the result of science. In case of illness modern man has recourse to physicians, to medical science. In case of economic and political affairs, he makes use of the results of psychological, social, economic and political sciences, and so on. Nobody reckons with direct intervention by transcendent powers.

Of course, there are today some survivals and revivals of primitive thinking and superstition. But the preaching of the Church would make a disastrous mistake if it looked to such revivals and conformed to them. The nature of man is to be seen in modern literature, as, for instance, in the novels of Thomas Mann, Ernst Jünger, Thornton Wilder, Ernest Hemingway, William Faulkner, Graham Greene and Albert Camus, or in the plays of Jean-Paul Sartre, Jean Anouilh, Jean Giraudoux, etc. Or let us think simply of the newspapers. Have you read anywhere in them that political or social or economic events are performed by supernatural powers such as God, angels or demons? Such events are always ascribed to natural powers, or to good or bad will on the part of men, or to human wisdom or stupidity.

The science of today is no longer the same as it was in the nineteenth century, and to be sure, all the results of science are relative, and no world-view of yesterday or today or tomorrow is definitive. The main point, however, is not the concrete results of scientific research and the contents of a world-view, but the method of thinking from which world-views follow. For example, it makes no difference in principle whether the earth rotates round the sun or the sun rotates round the earth, but it does make a decisive difference that modern man understands the motion of the universe as a motion which obeys a cosmic law, a law of nature which human reason can discover. Therefore, modern man acknowledges as reality only such phenomena or events as are comprehensible within the framework of the rational order of the universe. He does not acknowledge miracles because they do not fit into

37

this lawful order. When a strange or marvelous accident occurs, he does not rest until he has found a rational cause.

The contrast between the ancient world-view of the Bible and the modern world-view is the contrast between two ways of thinking, the mythological and the scientific. The method of scientific thinking and inquiry is in principle the same today as it was at the beginning of methodical and critical science in ancient Greece. It begins with the question about the ἀρχή (origin) from which the world is conceivable as unity, as κόσμος, as systematic order and harmony. It begins therefore also with the attempt to give reasonable proofs for every statement (λόγον διδόναι). These principles are the same in modern science, and it does not matter that the results of scientific research are changing over and over again, since the change itself results from the permanent principles.

Certainly it is a philosophical problem whether the scientific world-view can perceive the whole reality of the world and of human life. There are reasons for doubting whether it can do so, and we shall have to say more about this problem in the following chapters. But for present purposes it is enough to say that the thinking of modern men is really shaped by the scientific world-view, and that modern men need it for their daily lives.

· 2 ·

Therefore, it is mere wishful thinking to suppose that the ancient world-view of the Bible can be renewed. It is the radical abandonment and the conscious critique of the mythological world-view of the Bible which bring the real stumbling-block into sharp focus. This stumbling-block is that the Word of God calls man out of all man-made security. The scientific world-view engenders a great temptation, namely, that man strive for mastery over the world and over his own life. He knows the laws of nature and can use the powers of nature according to his plans and desires. He discovers more and more accurately the laws of social and of economic life, and thus organizes the life of the community more and more effectively—as Sophocles said in the famous chorus from *Antigone*

> Many wonders there be,
> but nought more wondrous than man.
> (332-333)

Thus modern man is in danger of forgetting two things: first, that his plans and undertakings should be guided not by his own desires for happiness and security, usefulness and profit, but rather by obedient response to the challenge of goodness, truth and love, by obedience to the commandment of God which man forgets in his selfishness and presumption; and secondly, that it is an illusion to suppose that real security can be gained by men organizing their own personal and community life. There are encounters and destinies which man cannot master. He cannot secure endurance for his works. His life is fleeting and its end is death. History goes on and pulls down all the towers of Babel again and again. There is no real, definitive security,

39

and it is precisely this illusion to which men are prone to succumb in their yearning for security.

What is the underlying reason for this yearning? It is the sorrow, the secret anxiety which moves in the depths of the soul at the very moment when man thinks that he must obtain security for himself.

It is the word of God which calls man away from his selfishness and from the illusory security which he has built up for himself. It calls him to God, who is beyond the world and beyond scientific thinking. At the same time, it calls man to his true self. For the self of man, his inner life, his personal existence is also beyond the visible world and beyond rational thinking. The Word of God addresses man in his personal existence and thereby it gives him freedom from the world and from the sorrow and anxiety which overwhelm him when he forgets the beyond. By means of science men try to take possession of the world, but in fact the world gets possession of men. We can see in our times to what degree men are dependent on technology, and to what degree technology brings with it terrible consequences. To believe in the Word of God means to abandon all merely human security and thus to overcome the despair which arises from the attempt to find security, an attempt which is always vain.

Faith in this sense is both the demand of and the gift offered by preaching. Faith is the answer to the message. Faith is the abandonment of man's own security and the readiness to find security only in the unseen beyond, in God. This means that faith is security where no security can be seen; it is, as Luther said, the readiness to enter confidently into the darkness of the future. Faith in God who has power over time and eternity, and who calls me and who has acted and now is acting on me—this faith can become real only in its "nevertheless" against the world. For in the world nothing of God and of His action is visible or can be visible to men who seek security in the world. We may say that the Word of God addresses man in his insecurity and calls him into freedom, for man loses his freedom in his very yearning for security. This formulation may sound paradoxical, but it becomes clear when we consider the meaning of freedom.

Genuine freedom is not subjective arbitrariness. It is freedom in obedience. The freedom of subjective arbitrariness is a delusion, for it delivers man up to his drives, to do in any moment what lust and passion dictate. This hollow freedom is in reality dependence on the lust and passion of the moment. Genuine freedom is freedom from the motivation of the moment; it is freedom which withstands the clamor and pressure of momentary motivations. It is possible only when conduct is determined by a motive which transcends the present moment, that is, by law. Freedom is obedience to a law of which the validity is recognized and accepted, which man recognizes as the law of his own being. This can only be a law which has its origin and reason in the beyond. We may call it the law of spirit or, in Christian language, the law of God.

This idea of freedom, constituted by law, this free

41

obedience or obedient freedom was well known both to ancient Greek philosophy and to Christianity. In modern times, however, this conception vanished and was replaced by the illusory idea of freedom as subjective arbitrariness which does not acknowledge a norm, a law from beyond. There ensues a relativism which does not acknowledge absolute ethical demands and absolute truths. The end of this development is nihilism.

There are several reasons for this development. The first is the development of science and technology which procures the illusion that man is master over the world and his life. Then there is the historical relativism which grew out of the Romantic Movement. It contends that our reason does not perceive eternal or absolute truths but is subject to historical development, that every truth has only a relative validity for a given time, race or culture, and thus, in the end, the search for truth becomes meaningless.

There is still another reason for the change from genuine freedom to the freedom of subjectivism. This deepest reason is anxiety in the face of real freedom, the yearning for security. Genuine freedom, it is true, is freedom within laws, but it is not freedom in security, because it is always freedom gained in responsibility and decision, and therefore it is freedom in insecurity. Freedom of subjective arbitrariness believes itself to be secure precisely because it is not responsible to a transcendent power, because it believes itself to be master of the world through science and technology. Subjective freedom grows out of the desire for security; it is in fact anxiety in the face of genuine freedom.

Now it is the Word of God which calls man into genuine freedom, into free obedience, and the task of de-mythologizing has no other purpose but to make clear the call of the Word of God. It will interpret the Scripture, asking for the deeper meaning of mythological conceptions and freeing the Word of God from a by-gone world-view.

·3·

Thus it follows that the objection is raised by a mistake, namely, the objection that de-mythologizing means rationalizing the Christian message, that de-mythologizing dissolves the message into a product of human rational thinking, and that the mystery of God is destroyed by de-mythologizing. Not at all! On the contrary, de-mythologizing makes clear the true meaning of God's mystery. The incomprehensibility of God lies not in the sphere of theoretical thought but in the sphere of personal existence. Not what God is in Himself, but how he acts with men, is the mystery in which faith is interested. This is a mystery not to theoretical thought, but to the natural wills and desires of men.

God's Word is not a mystery to my understanding. On the contrary, I cannot truly believe in the Word without understanding it. But to understand does not mean to explain rationally. I can understand, for example, what friendship, love and faithfulness mean, and precisely by genuinely understanding I know that the friendship, love and faithfulness which I personally enjoy are a mystery which I cannot but thankfully receive. For I perceive them neither by my rational thinking, nor by psychological, nor by anthropological analysis but only in open readiness to personal encounters. In this readiness I can understand them in a certain way already before I am given them because my personal existence needs them. Then I understand them in searching for them, in asking for them. Nevertheless, the fact itself that my yearning is fulfilled, that a friend comes to me, remains a mystery.

In the same manner I can understand what God's grace means, asking for it as long as it does not come to me, accepting it thankfully when it does come to me. The fact that it comes to me, that the gracious God is my God, remains forever a mystery, not because God performs in an irrational manner something that interrupts the natural course of events, but because it is inconceivable that He should encounter me in His Word as the gracious God.

IV

Modern Biblical Interpretation

and Existentialist Philosophy

·1·

Over and over again I hear the objection that de-mythologizing transforms Christian faith into philosophy. This objection arises from the fact that I call de-mythologizing an interpretation, an existentialist interpretation, and that I make use of conceptions developed especially by Martin Heidegger in existentialist philosophy.

We can understand the problem best when we remember that *de-mythologizing is an hermeneutic method*, that is, a method of interpretation, of exegesis. "Hermeneutics" means the art of exegesis.

Reflection on the art of hermeneutics has been increasingly neglected, at least in German theology, since Schleiermacher, who himself was interested in it and wrote important treatises on it. Only since the first World War has the interest in hermeneutics revived, when the work of the great German philosopher Wilhelm Dilthey became effective.*

Reflection on hermeneutics (the method of interpretation) makes it clear that interpretation, that is, exegesis, is always based on principles and conceptions which guide exegesis as presuppositions, although interpreters are often not aware of this fact.

To illustrate the point we may take as an example the understanding of the New Testament conception of "spirit" ($\pi\nu\epsilon\tilde{\upsilon}\mu\alpha$). During the nineteenth century the philosophies of Kant and Hegel profoundly influenced theologians and shaped their anthropological and ethical conceptions. Therefore, "spirit" in the New Testament was understood to mean spirit in the idealistic sense, based on the tradition of humanistic thinking which goes back to Greek idealistic philosophy. "Spirit" was thus understood to be the power of reason ($\lambda\acute{o}\gamma o\varsigma$, $\nu o\tilde{\upsilon}\varsigma$), in the inclusive sense as the power which works not only in rational thinking, in logic, but also in ethics, in moral judgments and behaviour and in the field of art and of poetry. "Spirit" was thought of as dwelling in the soul of men. In a certain sense spirit was thought

* As an example I may call attention to the great work of Joachim Wach, *Das Verstehen*, Vols. I-III (Leipzig, 1926-33). The more recent book by Christian Hartlich and Walter Sachs, *Der Ursprung des Mythosbegriffes in der modernen Bibelwissenschaft* (Tübingen, 1952) is especially important for our problem.

to be a power from beyond, from beyond the individual subject. The spirit within the soul was a part of the divine spirit which was cosmic reason. Therefore the spirit was for the individual subject the guide to living a truly human life. Man had to realize by education the possibilities given him by the spirit. This conception was generally dominant in philosophy as well as in theology during the nineteenth century.

The conception of "spirit" in the New Testament, especially in the Pauline epistles, was understood in this sense that spirit is the power of moral judgment and behaviour; and the attribute "holy" was understood in the sense of moral purity. Further, spirit was understood as the power of knowledge from which creedal and dogmatic statements grow. Of course, the spirit was thought to be the gift of God, but it was understood in the idealistic sense. Then Hermann Gunkel, in his little book *Die Wirkungen des Heiligen Geistes* (1st ed. 1888), pointed out the error of this interpretation. He showed that "spirit" in the New Testament means a divine power which does not belong to the human soul or reason but which is supernatural, a surprising, amazing power which causes marvellous psychological phenomena such as glossolalia, prophecy, etc. While the earlier interpretation was guided by idealistic conceptions, Gunkel's was guided by psychological conceptions. Psychological conceptions dominated the so-called *religionsgeschichtliche Schule* in general. Because these scholars were aware of psychological phenomena they recognized important thoughts

47

in the New Testament which had hitherto been over-looked or undervalued. They recognized, for example, the importance of enthusiastic and cultic piety and of cultic assemblies; they understood in a new way the conception of knowledge (γνῶσις) which as a rule does not mean theoretical, rational knowledge, but mystical intuition or vision, a mystical union with Christ. In this respect Wilhelm Bousset's *Kyrios Christos* (1st ed. 1913) was a landmark in New Testament research.

I need not continue this review. It will be clear that *every interpreter brings with him certain conceptions, perhaps idealistic or psychological, as presuppositions of his exegesis,* in most cases unconsciously. But then the question arises, which conceptions are right and adequate? Which presuppositions are right and adequate? Or is it perhaps impossible to give an answer to these questions?

I may illustrate the embarrassment (ἀπορία) by a further example. According to Paul, the believer who has received baptism is free from sin; he can no longer commit sin. "We know that our old self was crucified with him [i.e., by baptism] so that the sinful body might be destroyed, and we might no longer be enslaved to sin. For he who has died is freed from sin" (Rom. 6:6-7). How must we then understand the warnings and admonitions against sin contained in Paul's exhortations? How can the imperative "you shall not sin" be reconciled with the indicative "you are freed from sin"? Paul Wernle's book *Der Christ und die Sünde bei Paulus* (1897) gave the answer that they cannot

48

be reconciled; there is a contradiction in Paul; in theory all Christians are free from sin, but in practice Christians still commit sin, and therefore Paul must make exhortations. But is Wernle right? Is it possible to attribute to Paul such a contradiction? I do not think so. For Paul there is an inner connection between indicative and imperative, since in some sayings he lays stress on the connection. For example, "Cleanse out the old leaven that you may be fresh dough, as you really are unleavened" (I Cor. 5:7); or: "If we live by the Spirit, let us also walk by the Spirit" (Gal. 5:25). These sayings show clearly, it seems to me, the inner connection between indicative and imperative, namely, that the indicative is the ground of the imperative.

Now we return to our question: Which are the right conceptions? Which are the adequate presuppositions, if they are available at all? Should we perhaps say that we must interpret without any presupposition; that the text itself provides the conceptions of exegesis? This is sometimes asserted, but it is impossible. To be sure, our exegesis must be without presuppositions with regard to the results of our exegesis. We cannot know in advance what the text will say; on the contrary, we must learn from it. An exegesis which, for example, makes the presupposition that its results must agree with some dogmatic statement is not a real and fair exegesis. There is, however, a difference in principle between presuppositions in respect of results and presuppositions in respect of method. It can be said that method is nothing other than a kind of questioning, a way of putting questions. This means that I cannot understand a given text without asking certain questions of it. The questions may differ very widely. If you are interested in psychology, you will read the Bible—or any other literature—asking questions about psychological phenomena. You may read texts to gain knowledge of individual or of social psychology, or of the psychology of poetry, of religion, of technology, etc.

In this case you have certain conceptions by which you understand psychological life and by which you interpret the texts. Whence do you obtain these conceptions? This question calls attention to another important fact, to another presupposition of interpretation. You obtain the conceptions from your own psychical life. The resulting or corresponding presupposition of exegesis is that you do have a relation to the subject-matter (Sache)—in this case to the psychical life—about which you interrogate a given text. I call this relation the "life-relation." In this relation you have a certain understanding of the matter in question, and from this understanding grow the conceptions of exegesis. From reading the texts you will learn, and your understanding will be enriched and corrected. Without such a relation and such previous understanding (Vorverständnis) it is impossible to understand any text.

It is easy to see that you cannot understand any text of which the theme is music unless you are musical. You cannot understand a paper or a book on mathematics unless you can think mathematically, or a book on philosophy unless you can think philosophically. You cannot understand an historical text unless you yourself live historically and can therefore understand the life of history, that is, the powers and motives which give content and motion to history as the will to power, the state, laws, etc. You cannot understand a novel unless you know from your own life what love or friendship, hate or jealousy, etc., are.

This is, then, the basic presupposition for every form of exegesis: that your own relation to the subject-matter prompts the question you bring to the text and elicits the answers you obtain from the text.

I have tried to analyze the situation of the interpreter by using the example of psychological interpretation. You can read and interpret a text with other interests, for example, with aesthetical or with historical interest, with the interest in political or cultural history of states, etc. With regard to historical interpretation there are two possibilities. First, your interest may be to give a picture of a past time, to reconstruct the past; second, your interest may be to learn from historical documents what you need for your present practical life. For example, you can interpret Plato as an interesting figure of the culture of fifth-century Athenian Greece, but you can also interpret Plato to learn through him the truth about human life. In the latter case your interpretation is not motivated by interest in a past epoch of history, but by your search for the truth.

Now, when we interpret the Bible, what is our interest? Certainly the Bible is an historical document and

51

we must interpret the Bible by the methods of historical research. We must study the language of the Bible, the historical situation of the biblical authors, etc. But what is our true and real interest? Are we to read the Bible only as an historical document in order to reconstruct an epoch of past history for which the Bible serves as a "source"? Or is it more than a source? I think our interest is really to hear what the Bible has to say for our actual present, to hear what is the truth about our life and about our soul.

· 2 ·

Now the question arises as to which is the adequate method, which are the adequate conceptions? And also, which is the relation, the "life-relation," which we have in advance, to the theme (*Sache*) of the Bible from which our questions and our conceptions arise? Must we say that we do not have such relation in advance, since the theme of the Bible is the revelation of God, and we can gain a relation to God only by His revelation and not in advance of it?

Indeed, there are theologians who have argued in this manner, but it seems to me that they are in error. Man does have in advance a relation to God which has found its classical expression in the words of Augustine: "Tu nos fecisti ad te, et cor nostrum inquietum **est, donec requiescat in te**" (Thou hast made us for Thyself, and our heart is restless, until it rests in Thee). Man has a knowledge of God in advance, though not of the revelation of God, that is, of His action in Christ.

He has a relation to God in his search for God, conscious or unconscious. Man's life is moved by the search for God because it is always moved, consciously or unconsciously, by the question about his own personal existence. The question of God and the question of myself are identical.

Now we have found the adequate way to put the question when we interpret the Bible. This question is, *how is man's existence understood in the Bible*? I approach the Biblical texts with this question for the same reason which supplies the deepest motive for all historical research and for all interpretation of historical documents. It is that by understanding history I can gain an understanding of the possibilities of human life and thereby of the possibilities of my own life. The ultimate reason for studying history is to become conscious of the possibilities of human existence.

The interpretation of the Biblical scriptures, however, has a special motive. The tradition and the preaching of the Church tells us that we are to hear in the Bible authoritative words about our existence. What distinguishes the Bible from other literature is that in the Bible a certain possibility of existence is shown to me not as something which I am free to choose or to refuse. Rather, the Bible becomes for me a word addressed personally to me, which not only informs me about existence in general, but gives me real existence. This, however, is a possibility on which I cannot count in advance. It is not a methodological presupposition by means of which I can understand the Bible. For this possibility can become a reality only when I understand the word.

Our task, therefore, is to discover the hermeneutical principle by which we can understand what is said in the Bible. It is not permissible to evade this question, since in principle every historical document raises it, namely, what possibility of understanding human existence is shown and offered in each document of the Bible? In critical study of the Bible I can do no more than search for an answer to this question. It is beyond the competence of critical study that I should hear the word of the Bible as a word addressed personally to me and that I should believe in it. This personal understanding, in traditional terminology, is imparted by the Holy Spirit, who is not at my disposal. On the other hand, we can discover the adequate hermeneutical principle, the right way to ask the right questions, only by objective, critical reflection. If it is true that the right questions are concerned with the possibilities of understanding human existence, then it is necessary to discover the adequate conceptions by which such understanding is to be expressed. To discover these conceptions is the task of philosophy.

But now the objection is brought forward that exegesis falls under the control of philosophy. This is the case indeed, but we must ask in what sense it is so. It is an illusion to hold that any exegesis can be independent of secular conceptions. Every interpreter is inescapably dependent on conceptions which he has inherited from a tradition, consciously or unconsciously, and every tradition is dependent on some philosophy or other. In this way, for example, much of the exegesis of the nineteenth century was dependent on idealistic philosophy and on its conceptions, on its understanding of human existence. Such idealistic conceptions still influence many interpreters today. It follows, then, that historical and exegetical study should not be practiced without reflection and without giving an account of the conceptions which guide the exegesis. In other words, the question of the "right" philosophy arises.

·3·

At this point we must realize that there will never be a right philosophy in the sense of an absolutely perfect system, a philosophy which could give answers to all questions and clear up all riddles of human existence. Our question is simply which philosophy today offers the most adequate perspective and conceptions for understanding human existence. Here it seems to me that we should learn from existentialist philosophy, because in this philosophical school human existence is directly the object of attention.

We would learn little if existential philosophy, as many people suppose, attempted to offer an ideal pattern of human existence. The concept of "truth of existence" (*Eigentlichkeit*) does not furnish such a pattern. Existentialist philosophy does not say to me "in such and such a way you must exist"; it says only "you must exist"; or, since even this claim may be too large, it shows me what it means to exist. Existentialist

55

philosophy tries to show what it means to exist by distinguishing between man's being as "existence" and the being of all worldly beings which are not "existing" but only "extant" (*vorhanden*). (This technical use of the word "existence" goes back to Kierkegaard.) Only men can have an existence, because they are historical beings. That is to say, every man has his own history. Always his present comes out of his past and leads into his future. He realizes his existence if he is aware that each "now" is the moment of free decision: What element in his past is to retain value? What is his responsibility toward his future, since no one can take the place of another? No one can take another's place, since every man must die his own death. In his loneliness every man realizes his existence.

Of course, I cannot here carry out the existentialist analysis in detail. It may be enough to say that existentialist philosophy shows human existence to be true only in the act of existing. Existentialist philosophy is far from pretending that it secures for man a self-understanding of his own personal existence. For this self-understanding of my very personal existence can only be realized in the concrete moments of my "here" and "now." Existentialist philosophy, while it gives no answer to the question of my personal existence, makes personal existence my own personal responsibility, and by doing so it helps to make me open to the word of the Bible. It is clear, of course, that existentialist philosophy has its origin in the personal-existential question about existence and its possibilities. For how could it know about existence except from its own existential awareness, provided that existentialist philosophy is not identified with traditional anthropology? Thus it follows that existentialist philosophy can offer adequate conceptions for the interpretation of the Bible, since the interpretation of the Bible is concerned with the understanding of existence.

Once again we ask, does the existentialist understanding of existence and the existentialist analysis of that understanding already include a decision in favor of a particular understanding? Certainly such a decision is included, but what decision? Precisely the decision of which I have already spoken: "You must exist." Without this decision, without the readiness to be a human being, a person who in responsibility takes it upon himself to be, no one can understand a single word of the Bible as speaking to his own personal existence. While this decision does not require philosophical knowledge, scientific interpretation of the Bible does require the existentialist conceptions in order to explain the Biblical understanding of human existence. Thus only does it become clear that the hearing of the word of the Bible can take place only in personal decision.

That existentialist philosophy does not furnish a pattern of ideal existence may be illustrated by an example. Existentialist analysis describes particular phenomena of existence, for example, the phenomenon of love. It would be a misunderstanding to think that the existentialist analysis of love can lead me to understand how I must love here and now. The existentialist analysis can do nothing more than make it clear to me that I can understand love only by loving. No analysis can take the place of my duty to understand my love as an encounter in my own personal existence.

To be sure, philosophical analysis presupposes the judgment that it is possible to analyze human existence without reflection on the relation between man and God. But to understand human existence in its relation to God can only mean to understand my personal existence, and philosophical analysis does not claim to instruct me about my personal self-understanding. The purely formal analysis of existence does not take into account the relation between man and God, because it does not take into account the concrete events of the personal life, the concrete encounters which constitute personal existence. If it is true that the revelation of God is realized only in the concrete events of life here and now, and that the analysis of existence is confined to man's temporal life with its series of here and now, then this analysis unveils a sphere which faith alone can understand as the sphere of the relation between man and God.

The judgment that man's existence can be analyzed without taking into account his relation with God may be called an existential decision, but the elimination is not a matter of subjective preference; it is grounded in the existential insight that the idea of God is not at our disposal when we construct a theory of man's existence. Moreover, the judgment points to the idea of absolute freedom, whether this idea be accepted as true or rejected as absurd. We can also put it this way: that the elimination of man's relation with God is the expression of my personal knowledge of myself, the acknowledgment that I cannot find God by looking at or into myself. Thus, this elimination itself gives to the analysis of existence its neutrality. In the fact that existentialist philosophy does not take into account the relation between man and God, the confession is implied that I cannot speak of God as my God by looking into myself. My personal relation with God can be made real by God only, by the acting God who meets me in His Word.

V

The Meaning of God as Acting

It is often said that it is impossible to carry through de-mythologizing consistently, since, if the message of the New Testament is to be retained at all, we are bound to speak of God as acting. In such speech there remains a mythological residue. For is it not mythological to speak of God as acting? This objection may also take the form that, since de-mythologizing as such is not consistent with speaking of God as acting, Christian preaching must always remain mythological as was the preaching of the New Testament in general. But are such arguments valid? We must ask whether we are really speaking mythologically when we speak of God as acting. We must ask in what case and under

60

what conditions is such speaking mythological. Let us consider how God's action is understood in mythological thinking.

In mythological thinking the action of God, whether in nature, history, human fortune, or the inner life of the soul, is understood as an action which intervenes between the natural, or historical, or psychological course of events; it breaks and links them at the same time. The divine causality is inserted as a link in the chain of the events which follow one another according to the causal nexus. This is meant by the popular notion that a miraculous event cannot be understood except as a miracle, that is, as the effect of a supernatural cause. In such thinking the action of God is indeed conceived in the same way as secular actions or events are conceived, for the divine power which effects miracles is considered as a natural power. In **fact, however, a miracle in the** sense of an action of God cannot be thought of as an event which happens on the level of secular (worldly) events. It is not visible, not capable of objective, scientific proof which is possible only within an objective view of the world. To the scientific, objective observer God's action is a mystery.

The thought of the action of God as an unworldly and transcendent action can be protected from misunderstanding only if it is not thought of as an action which happens between the worldly actions or events, but as happening within them. The close connection between natural and historical events remains intact as it presents itself to the observer. The action of God is hidden from every eye except the eye of faith. Only the so-called natural, secular (worldly) events are visible to every man and capable of proof. It is *within* them that God's hidden action is taking place.

If someone now insists that to speak in this sense of God as acting is to speak mythologically, I have no objection, since in this case myth is something very different from what it is as the object of de-mythologizing. When we speak of God as acting, we do not speak mythologically in the objectifying sense.

·2·

Now another question arises: If faith maintains that God's hidden action is at work within the chain of secular events, faith may be suspected of being pantheistic piety. As we reflect on this problem, we can further clarify the sense in which we must understand God's action. Faith insists not on the direct identity of God's action with worldly events, but, if I may be permitted to put it so, on the paradoxical identity which can be believed only here and now against the appearance of non-identity. In faith I can understand an accident with which I meet as a gracious gift of God or as His punishment, or as His chastisement. On the other hand, I can understand the same accident as a link in the chain of the natural course of events. If, for example, my child has recovered from a dangerous illness, I give thanks to God because He has saved my child. By faith I can accept a thought or a resolution as a divine inspiration without removing the thought or the resolution from its connection with psychological motivation. It is possible, for example, that a decision which seemed insignificant when I made it, is seen later on to have marked a decisive and fruitful "turning point" in my life. Then I give thanks to God who inspired the decision. The creedal belief in God as creator is not a guarantee given in advance by means of which I am permitted to understand any event as wrought by God. The understanding of God as creator is genuine only when I understand myself here and now as the creature of God. This existential understanding does not need to express itself in my consciousness as explicit knowledge. In any case the belief in the almighty God is not the conviction given in advance that there exists an almighty Being who is able to do all things. Belief in the almighty God is genuine only when it actually takes place in my very existence, as I surrender myself to the power of God who overwhelms me here and now. Once more this does not mean that the belief must express itself in my consciousness as explicit knowledge; it does mean, however, that the statements of belief are not general statements. For example, Luther's statement *terra ubique domini* is not genuine as a dogmatic statement but only here and now when spoken in the decision of my very existence. This distinction, I think, can be best understood today by one for whom the dogmatic statement has become doubtful, that is, in the misery of imprisonment in Russia.

We may conclude that pantheism is indeed a conviction given in advance, a general world-view (*Welt-*

anschauung), which affirms that every event in the
world is the work of God because God is immanent in
the world. Christian faith, by contrast, holds that God
acts on me, speaks to me, here and now. The Christian
believes this because he knows that he is addressed by
the grace of God which meets him in the Word of God,
in Jesus Christ. God's grace opens his eyes to see that
"in everything God works for good with those who love
him" (Rom. 8:28). This faith is not a knowledge
possessed once for all; it is not a general world-view.
It can be realized only here and now. It can be a living
faith only when the believer is always asking what God
is telling him here and now. **God's action generally, in**
nature and history, is hidden from the believer just as
much as from the non-believer. But in so far as he sees
what comes upon him here and now in the light of the
divine word, he can and must take it as God's action.
Pantheism can say "there divinity is working" with
regard to any event, whatever it may be, without taking
into account the importance of what happens for my
personal existence. Christian faith can only say, "I trust
that God is working here and there, but His action is
hidden, for it is not directly identical with the visible
event. What it is that He is doing I do not yet know,
and perhaps I never shall know it, but faithfully I trust
that it is important for my personal existence, and I
must ask what it is that God says to me. Perhaps it may
be only that I must endure and be silent."

What follows from all this? In faith I deny the closed
connection of the worldly events, the chain of cause

and effect as it presents itself to the neutral observer. I deny the interconnection of the worldly events not as mythology does, which by breaking the connection places supernatural events into the chain of natural events; I deny the worldly connection as a whole when I speak of God. I deny the worldly connection of events when I speak of myself, for in this connection of worldly events, my self, my personal existence, my own personal life, is no more visible and capable of proof than is God as acting.

In faith I realize that the scientific world-view does not comprehend the whole reality of the world and of human life, but faith does not offer another general world-view which corrects science in its statements on its own level. Rather faith acknowledges that the world-view given by science is a necessary means for doing our work within the world. Indeed, I need to see the worldly events as linked by cause and effect not only as a scientific observer, but also in my daily living. In doing so there remains no room for God's working. This is the paradox of faith, that faith "nevertheless" understands as God's action here and now an event which is completely intelligible in the natural or historical connection of events. This "nevertheless" is inseparable from faith. This "nevertheless" (the German *dennoch* of Ps. 73:23; and Paul Tillich's *in spite of*) is inseparable from faith. Only this is real faith in miracle. He who thinks that it is possible to speak of miracles as of demonstrable events capable of proof offends against the thought of God as acting in hidden ways. He subjects God's action to the control of objective observation. He delivers up the faith in miracles to the criticism of science and in so doing validates such criticism.

·3·

Here another question arises. If God's action must be thought of as hidden, how is it possible to speak of it except in purely negative statements? Is the conception of transcendence an exclusively negative conception? It would be if to speak of God did not also mean to speak of our personal existence. If we speak of God as acting in general, transcendence would indeed be a purely negative conception, since every positive description of transcendence transposes it into this world. It is wrong to speak of God as acting in general statements, in terms of the formal analysis of man's existence. It is precisely the formal, existentialist analysis of human existence which shows that it is indeed impossible to speak of our personal existence in general statements. I can speak of my personal existence only here and now in the concrete situation of my life. To be sure, I can explicate in general statements the meaning, the sense of the conception of God and of God's action in so far as I can say that God is the power which bestows upon me life and existence, and in so far as I can describe these actions as the encounter which demands my own personal decision. By doing so I acknowledge that I cannot speak of God's action in general statements; I can speak only of what He does here and now with me, of what He speaks here and now to me. Even

66

if we do not speak of God in general terms but rather of His action here and now on us, we must speak in terms of general conceptions, for all of our language employs conceptions, but it does not follow that the issue in hand is a general one.

·4·

Now we may ask once more whether it is possible to speak of God as acting without falling into mythological speech. It is often asserted that the language of the Christian faith must of necessity be mythological language. This assertion must be examined carefully. First, even if we concede that the language of faith is really the langauge of myth, we must ask how this fact affects the program of de-mythologizing. This concession is by no means a valid argument against de-mythologizing, for the language of myth, when it serves as the language of faith, loses its mythological sense. To speak, for example, of God as creator, no longer involves speaking of His creatorship in the sense of the old myth. Mythological conceptions can be used as symbols or images which are perhaps necessary to the language of religion and therefore also of the Christian faith. Thus it becomes evident that the use of mythological language, far from being an objection to de-mythologizing, positively demands it.

Second, the assertion that the language of faith needs the language of myth can be validated only if a further qualification is taken into account. If it is true that mythological conceptions are necessary as symbols or images, we must ask what it is that is now expressed by such symbols or images. Surely it is impossible that their meaning within the language of faith should be expressed in terms of mythological conceptions. Their meaning can and must be stated without recourse to mythological terms.

Third, to speak of God as acting does not necessarily mean to speak in symbols or images. Such speech must be able to convey its full, direct meaning. How, then, must we speak of God as acting if our speech is not to be understood as mythological speech? God as acting does not refer to an event which can be perceived by me without myself being drawn into the event as into God's action, without myself taking part in it as being acted upon. In other words, to speak of God as acting involves the events of personal existence. The encounter with God can be an event for man only here and now, since man lives within the limits of space and time. When we speak of God as acting, we mean that we are confronted with God, addressed, asked, judged, or blessed by God. Therefore, to speak in this manner is not to speak in symbols or images, but to speak analogically. For when we speak in this manner of God as acting, we conceive God's action as an analogue to the actions taking place between men. Moreover, we conceive the communion between God and man as an analogue to the communion between man and man.* It is in this analogical sense that we speak of God's love and

---

* See the discussion of analogy by the late Erich Frank in his *Philosophical Understanding and Religious Truth* (New York, 1945).

care for men, of His demands and of His wrath, of His promise and grace, and it is in this analogical sense that we call Him Father. We are not only justified in speaking thus, but we must do so, since now we are not speaking of an idea about God, but of God Himself. Thus, God's love and care, etc., are not images or symbols; these conceptions mean real experiences of God as acting here and now. Especially in the conception of God as Father the mythological sense vanished long ago. We can understand the meaning of the term Father as applied to God by considering what it means when we speak to our fathers or when our children speak to us as their fathers. As applied to God the physical import of the term father has disappeared completely; it expresses a purely personal relationship. It is in this analogical sense that we speak of God as Father.

From this view of the situation some important conclusions follow. First, only such statements about God are legitimate as express the existential relation between God and man. Statements which speak of God's actions as cosmic events are illegitimate. The affirmation that God is creator cannot be a theoretical statement about God as *creator mundi* in a general sense. The affirmation can only be a personal confession that I understand myself to be a creature which owes its existence to God. It cannot be made as a neutral statement, but only as thanksgiving and surrender. Moreover, statements which describe God's action as cultic action, for example, that He offered His Son as a sacrificial victim, are not legitimate, unless they are understood in a purely symbolic sense. Second, the so-called images which describe God as acting are legitimate only if they mean that God is a personal being acting on persons. Therefore, political and juridical conceptions are not permissible, unless they are understood purely as symbols.

·5·

At this point a really important objection arises. If what we have said is correct, does it not follow that God's action is deprived of objective reality, that it is reduced to a purely subjective, psychological experience (*Erlebnis*); that God exists only as an inner event in the soul, whereas faith has real meaning only if God exists outside the believer? Such objections are brought forward again and again, and the shades of Schleiermacher and Feuerbach are conjured up in this controversy. *Erlebnis* (psychological experience) was indeed a popular catchword in German theology before the first World War. Faith was often described as *Erlebnis*. It was on this catch-word that Karl Barth and the so-called dialectical theologians made an all-out attack.

When we say that to speak of God means to speak of our own personal existence, the meaning is a totally different one. The objection which I have just summarized suffers from a psychological misunderstanding of the life of the soul. From the statement that to speak of God is to speak of myself, it by no means follows that God is not outside the believer. (This would be the case only if faith is interpreted as a purely psychological

70

event.) When man is understood in the genuine sense
as an historical being which has its reality in concrete
situations and decisions, in the very encounters of
life,* it is clear, on the one hand, that faith, speaking
of God as acting, cannot defend itself against the charge
of being an illusion, and, on the other hand, that faith
does not mean a psychologically subjective event.

Is it enough to say that faith grows out of the encounter with the Holy Scriptures as the Word of God, that
faith is nothing but simple hearing? The answer is yes.
But this answer is valid only if the Scriptures are understood neither as a manual of doctrine nor as a record
of witnesses to a faith which I interpret by sympathy
and empathy. On the contrary, to hear the Scriptures
as the Word of God means to hear them as a word
which is addressed to me, as *kerygma*, as a proclamation. Then my understanding is not a neutral one, but
rather my response to a call. The fact that the word of
the Scriptures is God's Word cannot be demonstrated
objectively; it is an event which happens here and now.
God's Word is hidden in the Scriptures as each action
of God is hidden everywhere.

I have said that faith grows out of the encounters
which are the substance of our personal lives as historical lives. Its meaning is readily understood when we
reflect upon the simple phenomena of our personal
lives. The love of my friend, my wife, my children,

* Man is an historical being not only in so far as he is enmeshed
in the course of the world-history, but particularly in so far as he
has a personal history of his own.

meets me genuinely only here and now as an event. Such love cannot be observed by objective methods but only by personal experience and response. From the outside, for example, by psychological observation, it cannot be perceived as love, but only as an interesting detail of psychological processes which are open to different interpretations. Thus, the fact that God cannot be seen or apprehended apart from faith does not mean that He does not exist apart from faith.

We must remember, however, that the affirmations of faith in its relation to its object, to God, cannot be proved objectively. This is not a weakness of faith; it is its true strength, as my teacher Wilhelm Herrmann insisted. For if the relation between faith and God could be proved as the relation between subject and object in worldly situations can be proved, then He would be placed on the same level as the world, within which the demand for proof is legitimate.

May we then say that God has "proved" Himself by the "facts of redemption" (*Heilstatsachen*)? By no means. For what we call facts of redemption are themselves objects of faith and are apprehended as such only by the eye of faith. They cannot be perceived apart from faith, as if faith could be based on data in the same way as the natural sciences are based on data which are open to empirical observation. To be sure, the facts of redemption constitute the grounds of faith, but only as perceived by faith itself. The principle is the same in our personal relationship as persons with persons. Trust in a friend can rest solely on the personality of my friend which I can perceive only when I trust him. There cannot be any trust or love without risk. It is true, as Wilhelm Herrmann taught us, that the ground and the object of faith are identical. They are one and the same thing, because we cannot speak of what God is in Himself but only of what He is doing to us and with us.

·6·

Now another question can be answered. If we hold that God's action is not visible, not capable of proof; that the events of redemption cannot be demonstrated, that the spirit with which the believers are endowed is not an object visible to objective observation; if we hold that we can speak of all such matters only when we are concerned with our personal existence, then it can be said that faith is a new understanding of personal existence. In other words, God's action bestows upon us a new understanding of ourselves.

The objection may be raised that in this case the event of God's revelation is nothing but the occasion which gives us understanding of ourselves and that the occasion is not recognized as an action which occurs in our actual lives and transforms them. In short, revelation is not recognized as a wonder. Then, the objection goes on, nothing happens but understanding or consciousness of the self; the content of the self-understanding is a timeless truth; once perceived it remains valid without regard to the occasion, namely, revelation, which has given rise to it.

73

This objection is based on a confusion to which I have referred above (p. 66), i.e., self-understanding of personal existence is confused with the philosophical analysis of man. The existential understanding (*das Existentielle*) is confused with the existentialist understanding (*das Existential*). Of philosophical analysis it may well be said that its statements are statements of timeless truth, not answers to the questions of the actual moment. But it is precisely this philosophical analysis of man, the *existentialist* understanding, which shows that the self-understanding—the existential understanding—becomes realized only here and now as my own self-understanding. Philosophical analysis shows what existence in the abstract means. By contrast, existential, personal self-understanding does not say what existence means in the abstract, but points to my life as a concrete person in the here and now. It is an act of understanding in which my very self and the relationships in which I am involved are understood together.

Such existential, personal understanding need not take place on the level of consciousness, and this, indeed, is rare. But such personal self-understanding, albeit unconscious, dominates, or exercises a powerful influence upon, all our sorrows and cares, ambitions, joys and anxieties. Moreover, this personal self-understanding is put to the test, is called into question (*ist in Frage gestelt*) in every situation of encounter. As my life goes on, my self-understanding may prove inadequate or it may become clearer and deeper as the result

74

of further experiences and encounters. This change may be due to radical self-examination or it may occur unconsciously, when, for example, my life is led out of the darkness of distress into the light of happiness or when the opposite experience comes to me. Entering into decisive encounters I may achieve a totally new self-understanding as a result of the love which is bestowed upon me when, for example, I marry or make a new friend. Even a little child unconsciously manifests such self-understanding in so far as he realizes that he is a child and that he therefore stands in a special relationship to his parents. His self-understanding expresses itself in his love, trust, feeling of security, thankfulness, etc.

In my personal existence, I am isolated neither from my environment nor from my own past and future. When, for example, I achieve through love a new self-understanding, what takes place is not an isolated psychological act of coming to consciousness; my whole situation is transformed. In understanding myself, I understand other people and at the same time the whole world takes on a new character. I see it, as we say, in a new light, and so it really is a new world. I achieve a new insight into my past and my future. I recognize new demands and am open to encounters in a new manner. My past and future become more than pure time as it is marked on a calendar or timetable. Now it should be clear that I cannot possess this self-understanding as a timeless truth, a conviction accepted once and for all. For my new self-understanding, by its very nature, must be renewed day by day, so that I understand the imperative self which is included in it.

Mutatis mutandis we may here apply the saying, "if we live by the Spirit, let us also walk by the Spirit" (Gal. 5:25). For indeed the saying is applicable to the self-understanding of faith, which is a response to our encounter with the word of God. In faith man understands himself anew. As Luther says in his interpretation of the Epistle to the Romans, "God going out from Himself brings it about that we go into ourselves; and making Himself known to us, He makes us known to ourselves." In faith man understands himself ever anew. This new self-understanding can be maintained only as a continual response to the word of God which proclaims His action in Jesus Christ. It is the same in ordinary human life. The new self-understanding which grows out of the encounter of man with man can be maintained only if the actual relation between man and man is maintained. "The kindness of God is new every morning"; yes, provided I perceive it anew every morning. For this is not a timeless truth, like a mathematical statement. I can speak of the kindness of God which is new every morning only if I myself am renewed every morning.

These considerations in turn throw light on the paradoxical juxtaposition of indicative and imperative in Paul to which I just referred above (Gal. 5:25). We now see that the indicative calls forth the imperative. The indicative gives expression to the new self-understanding of the believer, for the statement "I am freed from sin" is not a dogmatic one, but an existential one. It is the believer's confession that his whole existence is renewed. Since his existence includes his will, the imperative reminds him that he is free from sin, provided that his will is renewed in obedience to the commandment of God.

· 7 ·

A further objection which may arise is that the future action of God is eliminated by de-mythologizing. I reply that it is precisely de-mythologizing which makes clear the true meaning of God as acting in the future. Faith includes free and complete openness to the future. Philosophical analysis of existence shows that openness to the future is an essential feature of man's existence. But can philosophical analysis endow the concretely existing man with the openness? By no means. It can no more do this than it can bestow existence upon us. Philosophical analysis, as Heidegger has shown, can do no more than explain that man, if he is willing to exist in a full personal sense, must be open to the future. It can call attention to the effect, stimulating or frightening, of this perception when it affirms that for philosophical analysis the future cannot be characterized otherwise than as nothing.

Therefore, free openness to the future is freedom to take anxiety upon ourselves (*Angstbereitschaft*), i.e., to decide for it. If it is true that the Christian faith involves free openness to the future, then it is freedom from anxiety in the face of the Nothing. For this free-

77

dom nobody can decide of his own will; it can only be given, in faith. Faith as openness to the future is freedom from the past, because it is faith in the forgiveness of sins; it is freedom from the enslaving chains of the past. It is freedom *from* ourselves as the old selves, and *for* ourselves as the new selves. It is freedom from the illusion, grounded in sin, that we can establish our personal existence through our own decision. It is the free openness to the future which Paul acclaims in saying that "death is swallowed up in victory" (I Cor. 15:54).

· 8 ·

Here a final and crucial question arises. If we must speak of God as acting only in the sense that He acts with me here and now, can we still believe that God has acted once for all on behalf of the whole world? Are we not in danger of eliminating this "once for all" of Paul's (Rom. 6:10)? Are we not in danger of relegating the divine dispensation, the history of salvation, to the dimension of timelessness? It should be clear from what we have said that we are not speaking of an idea of God but of the living God in whose hands our time lies, and who encounters us here and now. Therefore, we can make our answer to the objection in the single affirmation that God meets us in His Word, in a concrete word, the preaching instituted in Jesus Christ. While it may be said that God meets us always and everywhere, we do not see and hear Him always and everywhere, unless His Word supervenes and enables

78

us to understand the moment here and now, as Luther so often insisted. The idea of the omnipresent and almighty God becomes real in my personal existence only by His Word spoken here and now. Accordingly it must be said that the Word of God is what it is only in the moment in which it is spoken. The Word of God is not a timeless statement but a concrete word addressed to men here and now. To be sure God's Word is His eternal Word, but this eternity must not be conceived as timelessness, but as His presence always actualized here and now. It is His Word as an event, in an encounter, not as a set of ideas, not, for example, as a statement about God's kindness and grace in general, although such a statement may be otherwise correct, but only as addressed to me, as an event happening and meeting me as His mercy. Only thus is it the *verbum externum,* the word from the outside. Not as a knowledge possessed once for all, but precisely as meeting me over and over again is it really the *verbum externum.*

From this it follows that God's Word is a real word spoken to me in human language, whether in the preaching of the Church or in the Bible, in the sense that the Bible is not viewed merely as an interesting collection of sources for the history of religion, but that the Bible is transmitted through the Church as a word addressing us. This living Word of God is not invented by the human spirit and by human sagacity; it rises up in history. Its origin is an historical event, by which the speaking of this word, the preaching, is

79

rendered authoritative and legitimate. This event is Jesus Christ.

We may say that this assertion is paradoxical. For what God has done in Jesus Christ is not an historical fact which is capable of historical proof. The objectifying historian as such cannot see that an historical person (Jesus of Nazareth) is the eternal Logos, the Word. It is precisely the mythological description of Jesus Christ in the New Testament which makes it clear that the figure and the work of Jesus Christ must be understood in a manner which is beyond the categories by which the objective historian understands world-history, if the figure and the work of Jesus Christ are to be understood as the divine work of redemption. That is the real paradox. Jesus is a human, historical person from Nazareth in Galilee. His work and destiny happened within world-history and as such come under the scrutiny of the historian who can understand them as part of the nexus of history. Nevertheless, such detached historical inquiry cannot become aware of what God has wrought in Christ, that is, of the eschatological event.

According to the New Testament the decisive significance of Jesus Christ is that he—in his person, his coming, his passion, and his glorification—is the eschatological event. He is the one "who is to come," and we are not to "look for another" (Matt. 11:3). "When the time had fully come, God sent forth his Son" (Gal. 4:4). "This is the judgment, that the light has come into the world" (John 3:19). "The hour is coming, and now is, when the dead will hear the voice of the Son of God, and those who hear will live" (John 5:25). All these sayings declare that Jesus Christ is the eschatological event. The crucial question for de-mythologizing is whether this understanding of Jesus Christ as the eschatological event is inextricably bound up with the conceptions of cosmological eschatology as it is in the New Testament, with the single exception of the Fourth Gospel.

In the Fourth Gospel, as we have seen, the cosmological eschatology is understood, from our point of view, as an historical eschatology. We have also seen that for Paul the believer is already a new creation, "the old has passed away, behold, the new has come" (II Cor. 5:17). We must, therefore, say that to live in faith is to live an eschatological existence, to live beyond the world, to have passed from death to life (cf. John 5:24; I John 3:14). Certainly the eschatological existence is already realized in anticipation, for "we walk by faith, not by sight" (II Cor. 5:7). This means that the eschatological existence of the believer is not a worldly phenomenon, but is realized in the new self-understanding. This self-understanding, as we have seen before, grows out of the Word. The eschatological event which is Jesus Christ happens here and now as the Word is being preached (II Cor. 6:2; John 5:24) regardless of whether this Word is accepted or rejected. The believer has passed from death to life, and the unbeliever is judged; the wrath of God rests upon him, says John (John 3:18, 36; 9:39). The word of the preaching spreads death and life, says Paul (II Cor. 2:15f.).

Thus, the "once for all" is now understood in its

genuine sense, namely, as the "once for all" of the eschatological event. For this "once for all" is not the uniqueness of an historical event but means that a particular historical event, that is, Jesus Christ, is to be understood as the eschatological "once for all." As an eschatological event this "once for all" is always present in the proclaimed word, not as a timeless truth, but as happening here and now. Certainly the Word says to me that God's grace is a prevenient grace which has already acted for me; but not in such a way that I can look back on it as an historical event of the past. The acting grace is present now as the eschatological event. The word of God is Word of God only as it happens here and now. The paradox is that the word which is always happening here and now is one and the same with the first word of the apostolic preaching crystallized in the Scriptures of the New Testament and delivered by men again and again, the word whose content may be formulated in general statements. It cannot be the one without the other. This is the sense of the "once for all." It is the eschatological once-for-all because the word becomes event here and now in the living voice of the preaching.

The word of God and the Church belong together, because it is by the word that the Church is constituted as the community of the called, in so far as the preaching is not a lecture comprised of general propositions but the message which is proclaimed by authorized, legitimate messengers (II Cor. 5:18-20). As the word is God's word only as an event, the Church is genuine

Church only as an event which happens each time here and now; for the Church is the eschatological community of the saints, and it is only in a paradoxical way identical with the ecclesiastical institutions which we observe as social phenomena of secular history.

·9·

We have seen that the task of de-mythologizing received its first impulse from the conflict between the mythological views of the world contained in the Bible and the modern views of the world which are influenced by scientific thinking, and it has become evident that faith itself demands to be freed from any world-view produced by man's thought, whether mythological or scientific. For all human world-views objectivize the world and ignore or eliminate the significance of the encounters in our personal existence. This conflict shows that in our age faith has not yet found adequate forms of expression; that our age has not yet become aware of the identity of its ground and object; that it has not yet genuinely understood the transcendence and hiddenness of God as acting. It is not yet aware of its own "nevertheless," or of its "in spite of"; over and over again it yields to the temptation to objectivize God and His action. Therefore, the criticism of the mythological world-view of Biblical and ecclesiastical preaching renders a valuable service to faith, for it recalls faith to radical reflection on its own nature. The task of de-mythologizing has no other purpose than to take up this challenge. The invisibility of God excludes every

83

myth which tries to make God and His action visible; God withholds Himself from view and observation. We can believe in God only in spite of experience, just as we can accept justification only in spite of conscience. Indeed, de-mythologizing is a task parallel to that performed by Paul and Luther in their doctrine of justification by faith alone without the works of law. More precisely, de-mythologizing is the radical application of the doctrine of justification by faith to the sphere of knowledge and thought. Like the doctrine of justification, de-mythologizing destroys every longing for security. There is no difference between security based on good works and security built on objectifying knowledge. The man who desires to believe in God must know that he has nothing at his own disposal on which to build this faith, that he is, so to speak, in a vacuum. He who abandons every form of security shall find the true security. Man before God has always empty hands. He who gives up, he who loses every security shall find security. Faith in God, like faith in justification, refuses to single out qualified and definable actions as holy actions. Correspondingly, faith in God, like faith in creation, refuses to single out qualified and definable realms from among the observable realities of nature and history. Luther has taught us that there are no holy places in the world, that the world as a whole is indeed a profane place. This is true in spite of Luther's "the earth everywhere is the Lord's" (*terra ubique Domini*), for this, too, can be believed only in spite of all of the evidence. It is not the consecration of the priest but the proclaimed word which makes holy the house of God. In the same way, the whole of nature and history is profane. It is only in the light of the proclaimed word that what has happened or is happening here or there assumes the character of God's action for the believer. It is precisely by faith that the world becomes a profane place and is thus restored to its true place as the sphere of man's action.

Nevertheless, the world is God's world and the sphere of God as acting. Therefore, our relation to the world as believers is paradoxical. As Paul puts it in I Cor. 7:29-31, "Let those who have wives live as though they had none, and those who mourn as though they were not mourning, and those who rejoice as though they were not rejoicing, and those who buy as though they had no goods, and those who deal with the world as though they had no dealings with it." In terms of this book, we may say, "let those who have the modern world-view live as though they had none."

Indices

I · NAMES AND SUBJECTS

Aeschylus, 24

Anouilh, Jean, 37

Anti-Christ, 34

Apocalpytic, Jewish, 12, 26f., 33

Augustine, St., 52

Barth, Karl, 70

Bible: authority, 53f.
  interpretation of, 51ff., 57
  Word of God, 71, 79

Blessedness, eternal: and salvation, 27
  as obtaining grace and righteousness, 29
  as philosophical dialogue, 28f., 30
  gift of God, 12
  present in Christ, 32

Body: physical, 28, 29
  spiritual, 29

Bousset, Wilhelm, 48

Camus, Albert, 37

Causality: and faith, 64ff.
  mythological view of, 14f., 18f., 61

Causality—*Continued*
  scientific view of, 15f., 37f., 65

Christ: and the Church, 32
  parousia, 32, 33
  person and work, 80ff.
  resurrection, 32, 33
  revelation of God, 52
  Word of God, 76, 79f.

Church: and the Bible, 79
  and Christ, 32
  and the Word of God, 82f.
  eschatological community, 32, 83
  preaching, 13ff., 36, 78, 79, 82
  worship, 30, 31

Cross: stumbling-block, 36
  suffering of, 17

Daniel, Book of, 12

Death, 28, 30, 32, 39, 56

Demons: casting out of, 13
  place in mythology, 19
  Satan's army, 15

87

II · PASSAGES

A · Biblical

B · Classical